THE BATTLE AGAINST THE *Spirit* OF Impossibility

DR. D. K. OLUKOYA

Warfare Prayer Series 20

THE BATTLE AGAINST THE SPIRIT OF IMPOSSIBILITY

Dr. D. K. Olukoya

Published by:
The Battle Cry Christian Ministries
322, Herbert Macaulay Way, Yaba,
P. O. Box 12272, Ikeja, Lagos State, Nigeria.
Phone: 01 8044415, 0803-304-4239,
e-mail: sales@battlecryng.com
website: www.battlecryng.com

The Battle Against The Spirit of Impossibility

Published - June, 2005
Reprinted - June, 2011

©2005 Dr. D. K. Olukoya

ISBN 978-38233-1-0

All the Scriptures are from the King James Version

Cover illustration by: **Sister Shade Olukoya**

All rights reserved. No part of this publication may be reproduced, stored in a retrieval system, or transmitted in any form or by any means, electronic, mechanical, photocopying, recording or otherwise without the prior written permission of the publishers.

Printed in Nigeria.

TABLE OF CONTENTS

CHAPTER   PAGE

1 THE SPIRIT OF IMPOSSIBILITY 4

2 THE SCHOOL OF THE WITS' END 19

3 WHEN THE ENEMY IS AT LARGE 36

The Spirit Of Impossibility

The Lord Jesus made a proclamation in the gospel according to Matthew.

Matthew 19:22 - But when the young man heard that saying, he went away sorrowful: for he had great possessions.

THE SPIRIT OF IMPOSSIBILITY

Behind every human manifestation and operation or behind any problem and activity, there is a spirit.

Behind every hindrance and impossibility is a spirit.

There is a spirit known as the spirit of impossibility. This spirit hinders and attacks the human race. When the spirit of impossibility comes upon anyone, what is naturally possible for others becomes impossible. The spirit wages war against success, antagonizes breakthroughs and squanders fortunes. The spirit of impossibility will not prevent anyone from starting a project or a business, but it will make sure that it will not be successful. When the spirit of impossibility is in progress in the life of any person, anything he lays his hands upon will become a white elephant projects.

The spirit of impossibility is the spirit of abandonment. Many have abandoned projects that would have made them prosper. They began to pursue projects which the spirit of impossibility has incubated.

The spirit of impossibility makes use of various devices to frustrate people. The spirit of impossibility makes situations hopeless. It makes a project unrealizable and mountains insurmountable. When the spirit of impossibility engulfs a person, all efforts made in the area of prayer are empty words. A person who is under the attack of the spirit of impossibility can pray but he does not believe his prayers. As he prays, the hidden, subtle spirit of unbelief will remain in hiding in the laboratory of his heart.

A person who is possessed by the spirit of unbelief might pray and fast for three days and night. He might engage himself in fervent prayers backed up by serious fasting sessions. Immediately he has finished praying, the evil monster, the spirit of impossibility, will come with a challenge saying, "Do you think that it is simple to have your prayers answered". The spirit of impossibility will look at a situation or condition and declare "Un-fortunate"! "Un-achievable"! Impossible!

This is why the Bible lays a great deal of emphasis on faith. The Bible encourages us to have faith. Hence, it says,

Mark 11:23-24: For verily I say unto you, That whosoever shall say unto this mountain, Be thou removed, and be thou cast into the sea; and shall not doubt in his heart, but shall believe that those things which he saith shall come to pass; he shall have whatsoever he saith. Therefore I say unto you, What things soever ye desire, when ye pray, believe that ye receive them, and ye shall have them.

Please take note of the condition "Shall not doubt in his heart". What makes a man to doubt in his heart is the spirit of impossibility.

Oftentimes, people get frightened when they are told by medical experts that they would soon die based on medical reports. If these people can have faith and silence the spirit of impossibility, such medical reports will be rendered null and void.

AN AMAZING TESTIMONY

Let me share amazing testimony with you. A man got very sick in Nigeria and he was rushed abroad for medical treatment. He was reported to have had cancer. He underwent surgical operations. The doctor discovered that malignant cancer had destroyed his internal organs. The surgeon declared, "Excuse me sir, put your house in order because you have got a maximum of six weeks to live. You will soon die". What an evil report!

The man was flown back to Nigeria to enable him put his house in order before he died. Just when every hope was lost, one of the man's daughters who used to come to MFM brought him to the Church. As he sat in the service, a word of knowledge says, "There is a man who was brought to this meeting. You are suffering from cancer that has eaten up the whole of your internal organ. The power of the Lord will be made manifest in you now". The man did not believe anything because he only came to please his daughter who insisted that he should go for prayers. But, the man began to notice that his body was becoming stronger. The man did not die after six weeks. One year later, he was still alive. The man is still alive and healthy today.

The man then traveled to England not for medical treatment but for holidays. While he was on his way, he thought about checking up the doctor who told him he had six weeks to live. When he entered the room and the white doctor saw him, he was surprised that the man was still alive. Only God can arrest every problem sponsored by the spirit of impossibility.

Do not give in to the lies of the devil. Don't allow satan to tell you that your body is dead and that there is nothing that could be done about it. It does not matter if people are against you, if you can believe, victory shall yours in the name of Jesus.

Negative verdicts are mere challenges. Possibility thinkers will always believe in the positive side of life.

Satan and his agents can infiltrate x-ray of scan machines to alter and manipulate things. The devil can easily frame up lies that something is hidden in the parts of the body. You might ask, "How is it possible". The fact is that most of the medical instruments are operated by the unbelievers. The enemy could easily manipulate the instruments without much resistance from anyone who lacks fire.

NO UNCHANGEABLE VERDICT

According to divine mathematics, there is nothing like an everlasting problem. No verdict is unchangeable. Just as the enemy has his own verdict, God has His own verdict too. Man has his own verdict. It is only the verdict of God that is unchangeable. But then, even the legitimate verdict of God can be changed with the right display of repentance, determination, desperation faith and persistence.

On several occasions in the Bible, God changed His verdict. That is why God wants us to bring strong reasons and plead our cases before Him. God says that believers should bring strong reasons why the verdicts must be changed.

Isaiah 43:26 - Put me in remembrance: let us plead together: declare thou, that thou mayest be justified.

There are several people who are passing through stressful periods in their lives. There are some who are passing through their time of Jacob's trouble. Some are harassed by the enemy, while others are attacked through reproach. I have a word from God for you. God shall arise and the verdict of the enemy over your life shall be changed, in the name of Jesus.

If you can argue your case on the basis of the word of God, you can change the Lord's verdict. When David was confronted with the verdict of death, he said, "I shall not die but live to declare the glory of the Lord". He declared it and David lived.

IS ANYTHING TOO HARD?

You can change the negative verdict that men have issued against you. You can be what God wants you to be. You can have what God has promised you. Any verdict can be changed as it changed in favour of the Ninevites and Hezekiah the king. You can pack aside the opinion of the experts and hold on to God's report concerning your situation. The expert's opinion in any field does not cancel the opinion of the Almighty. The Bible comes up with a question in the book of Genesis.

Genesis 18:14 - Is any thing too hard for the LORD? At the time appointed I will return unto thee, according to the time of life, and Sarah shall have a son.

The question is "Is there anything too hard for the Lord"? What is provided as an answer to the question is raised in Jeremiah 32:17.

Jeremiah 32:17 - Ah Lord GOD! behold, thou hast made the heaven and the earth by thy great power and stretched out arm, and there is nothing too hard for thee:

The answer is, "There is nothing too hard for thee".

There is no promise too hard for God to fulfill. There is no prayer too hard for God to answer. God is not limited by circumstances. If God wants to work wonders, He will start in an unusual manner. When God wants to surprise the sons of men, He starts by making impossible situations possible.

A brother called me on phone from America. The brother happened to come from a very poor background. He wanted to read Medicine. He applied to the best schools in America. Miraculously, he secured admission into one of the best schools. He was asked to resume and pay up his school fees but be had nothing. Consequently, a letter was written to him that since he could not pay, his admission would be cancelled.

He cried bitterly to the Lord. When he called me on the phone, he was crying. I asked him a question, "Do you believe that God can do the impossible? "He said, "Yes sir, but this is America". I said, "Do you believe that God is the same everywhere?" He said, "Yes, I believe but I wish there is Prayer City here that I may go there and pray". I said, "Do you believe that you can create Prayer City in your living room"? He said, "Yes sir".

We prayed. The brother later applied to five schools. One school turned him down because he could not pay the school fees. On the second day the other four schools wrote to him and offered him scholarship. He had the problem of taking a decision on which one of the four options to choose from. The lesson here is that, when you believe that you are at your wit's end, the Lord will intervene on your behalf.

No problem is too hard for God. No situation too hard for God to solve or resolve. No enemy is too hard for God to deal with.

There is no mountain too high that God cannot remove. There is no reproach too intense for God to remove. There is no sickness too severe for God to eliminate. There is no enemy too clever for God to deal with.

AWESOME GOD!

God is a Spirit. He is the God of Abraham, Isaac and Jacob. He is the one who grants dreams, revelations and angelic visitations. He covered dry land with a deluge of water during the days of Noah. He constructed an expressway from the surface; so that children of Israel could pass through the Red Sea on dry land.

He is the one who sent rain, fire, hailstones, thunder and lightning from heavens to the earth, the Bible says. He brought water out of the rock. He was the one who made a snake out of Moses' rod. From darkness, He made light. From the dust, He made man. He sent fire on Elijah's altar. He was the one who caused Jeroboam's hand to wither while pointing to the prophet of God. He was the same God who turned Nebuccahadnezzar into an animal. He turned River Nile to blood. He made Jericho's wall to collapse.

A man was brought to a crusade paralysed. He was at the rear. As prayer was going on, the Spirit of God said. "Something is coming out of someone's head". He noticed that something was coming out of his head. He could not open his eyes to examine the structure because of the instruction of the man of God that all eyes should be closed.

He closed his eyes but grabbed what was coming out of his head. The structure resembled a long ruler. By the time the preacher ended the prayer saying, "In Jesus name we pray" he had brought out a tall ruler-like structure; he could not only walk, he could also run.

A demonic verdict was issued against the man. Each time he got to any hospital he was told that he wold never walk again. But one glorious day, God changed the doctor's verdict. It is my prayer for you that the confidence of the enemy over you, shall be broken, in the name of Jesus.

It was God who joined Meshach, Shedrach and Abednego in the fiery furnace in form of the "Fourth Man in the fire". He gave eyeball to the man who was born blind. He touched the tongue of the dumb man and the dumb began to speak. He touched the leg of the crippled and he began to walk. He programmed dreams into Joseph's life and he began to dream and interpret them.

He was the one who sent an angel to programme victory into the sword of Joshua. He sent angels to Egypt to visit the Egyptians with destruction.

He visited the disciples with tongues of fire on the day of Pentecost. He opened the prison doors and brought the disciples out of prison. The power of God is greater than any other power in the universe.

THE COUNTER ATTACK

There are things to do to destroy the spirit of impossibility. There are things you must avoid. There are prayers to pray and there are some actions to take. The truth of the matter is that the presence of the spirit of impossibility is as real as the air you breathe.

This explains why persons could do the same business, one will succeed and the other one fails. Two kinds of people may be subjected to the same conditions, one may succeed and the other one may fail because of the spirit of impossibility.

Do you want to stop the spirit of impossibility? You must take note of the following:

1. Stop incubating the spirit of impossibility: If you incubate the eggs of the spirit of impossibility, it will hatch. What does it take to incubate the spirit of impossibility? When in your heart, you entertain thoughts of failure, it means you are incubating the spirit of impossibility.

For example, if you sat for an examination in which you did not appear to have done well, the fact that you appeared not to have done well does not mean that you should score yourself very low in the examination. If you do that, it means you are incubating the spirit of impossibility, which is the spirit of failure.

The thoughts and actions of failure break down spiritual hedge and the spirit of impossibility moves in. Do not break the hedge of spirituality lest the serpent of impossibility bites you. Another way of incubating the spirit of impossibility is by meditating on the magnitude of your problem.

A woman came to a crusade in New York City. She brought a baby to the crusade. Immediately she sat before me, I asked, "What can I do to help you"? She said, "Man of God, I cannot talk. Please read this paper" She then gave me hospital report on her baby. According to the medical reports 26 kinds of sickness were troubling a six month old baby!

We started to pray. To the glory of God when I went there again, two years later I could no longer recognize the little boy. All of a sudden, one after the other sickness disappeared. But if we had started to meditate on the gravity of the problem, the baby she had would have died prematurely.

When you meditate on the magnitude of a problem it expands. You incubate the spirit of impossibility when you focus on the difficulty instead of the solution.

How do people incubate the spirit of impossibility? It is when you surrender to discouragement and you listen to the symptoms of the problem. If you want to see before you believe then you are under the influence of the spirit of impossibility. The Bible says that, you must believe before you see.

When you are seeking for a solution to your problems through other avenues apart from the word of God and prayer, then you are incubating the spirit of impossibility. When you are preoccupied with finding solutions to your problems, to the extent that you abandon God for other things, then you are incubating the spirit of impossibility. If you give up and start to entertain the thoughts of committing suicide, then you are incubating the spirit of impossibility.

Jesus has a glorious programme for your life. His programme is of peace and not of destruction.

2. Repent from all known sins: the reason for this is that, any sin in your life will only harden the enemy against you.

3. Reject the negative verdict: Do not agree with it.

4. Confront the power behind the negative verdict.

5. Pray verdict changing prayers.

When you do these things, God will move into your situation.

It is time for you to pray with faith in your heart and believe God, for there is nothing too hard for Him.

PRAYER POINTS

1. Spirit of impossibility, depart from my life and come back no more, in the name of Jesus.

2. Every curse and covenant of impossibility, break, in the name of Jesus.

3. Collective captivity of impossibility, die, in Jesus' name

4. Every root of impossibility, die, in the name of Jesus.

5. Red Sea of impossibility, be divided, in Jesus' name.

6. Oh God! arise and break me free from every evil company, in the name of Jesus.

7. Oh God arise and let every evil company vomit me, in the name of Jesus.

8. Oh God! Arise and break me free, from every company of stagnancy, in the name of Jesus.

9. Thou power of the night that is attacking my destiny, attack yourself, in the name of Jesus.

10. My Father, as you parted the Red Sea, separate affliction from my life, in the name of Jesus.

11. Every power of the night, ministering against me, scatter, in the name of Jesus.

12. Every satanic load placed upon my head in the dream, backfire, in the name of Jesus.

13. Any power, staying awake to harm me, die, in the name of Jesus.

14. Oh God, who makes the impossible possible, manifest your power in my life, in the name of Jesus.

The School Of The Wits' End

This message shall be taken from the book of Psalms.

Psalm 107:26-27: They mount up to the heaven, they go down again to the depths: their soul is melted because of trouble. They reel to and fro, and stagger like a drunken man, and are at their wits' end.

It is my prayer that your melted soul shall receive divine solution in the name of Jesus. Trouble can melt the soul. Trouble can make men to reel to and fro and stagger like drunkards.

There is a place called the wit's end. What is the wit's end? It is a place of termination of human wisdom and intelligence. It is a place where the thought of the way out has been lost. It is a place where you have done your best but there is no solution in view. It is a place where you witness the end of all human ability and resources. It is a point when you move back and forth and you do not know where else to go. It is a place where there is no human way of escape. It is a way where there is no help at sight. It is a place where there is no hope of deliverance. Have you arrived at or are you approaching your wit's end?

THE WITS' END

What is the understanding of the wit's end? It is a situation where there is no help. It is a situation where human help has proved inadequate; a situation where you simply do not know what to do again. It is a situation where all your helpers flee and you are on your own. It is a situation where it seems that every method has failed.

CATALOGUES OF PEOPLE AT WITS' END

There are many people who have arrived at their wits' end and the case is hopeless. There are many people in the word of God who arrived at their wits' end at a point in time. A good example is Moses, when he was standing by the Red Sea. Right there, there was no way forward. But the Lord told him "Look forward" Eventually, God cleared the sea and made the sea to stand as an impregnable wall and the children of God passed through a dry land.

Hezekiah also got to his wits' end. It was so terrible that Hezekiah cried out. Abraham arrived at his wits' end too. Abraham was old. His wife, too, was old. Yet, they were looking for a child. Daniel too was at his wits' end. Elisha at the bank of river Jordan got to his wits' end.

COMPLICATED CASES

I remember a terrible case involving a woman who had four children. She resolved to do "family planning" by removing her uterus is order to stop having children. One day as they traveled, a trailer ran into their car. All the four children died. The woman and her husband remained alive. There was no longer any hope, humanly speaking, of giving birth to children as her womb had been removed. The woman got to her wits' end. Her problem persisted until the Great Physician took over her problem.

The world is full of problems. What pushes people to their wits' end is a problem. There is no educator like problems. If you carefully watch people during the time of problems you will discover the kind of person they are. People display their real character when problems come up. There is no way you can run away from problems. There is no place you could run to and problem would not pursue you. If you travel out of your country and begin to live overseas, the moment you get there you will be confronted with problems.

The day of trouble comes unto every man. There is no way you can run away from trouble. Trouble and problems are very intelligent because they know the address of everyone. By the mathematics of God, strong men grow through problems. Sometimes, problems come to a person as a result of progress made. There is no system that does not develop a crisis. Any system that does not develop a crisis is never a good one. In fact, it is not a system in the real sense of the word.

BENEFITS OF TROUBLE

God's best soldiers are trained in the school of affliction. If you are a good reader of the Bible, you will discover that one of the observations which you could make about men of God in the Bible is that they all got into one problem or the other. Abraham, Daniel, Joseph, David, Elijah, Elisha, and so on fell into one trouble or the other.

Daniel got into trouble for praying. Joseph got into trouble because of his dreams and he entered into another trouble because he did not want to commit sin. By God's mathematics, what a man needs to get on course and move ahead is a powerful enemy. When the enemy waxes stronger, then you must begin to pray. As you pray, your spiritual muscle begins to grow. The enemy will then become instrumental to activating your breakthroughs.

There is a special place reserved for anyone who does not want problems at all. The special place is the cemetery. There are no problems for those who "lie in state" at the cemetery. Those who claim that they have no problem have the greatest problems on earth. When you see them, you will shake your head out of pity. The problems of such people have become compounded because they cannot see the battle confronting them.

Jesus never deceived us. He promised all his followers three major things:

1. Constant trouble
2. Constant joy
3. His abiding presence

In God's mathematics, problems can prepare ordinary Christians for extra ordinary services. Life's greatest problems can become life's greatest blessings. Are you discouraged and tired of everything? Perhaps you have prayed and interceded, you might have subjected yourself to deliverance ministry several times and yet the solution is yet to be visible. This shows that you are at your wits' end.

The stones that the devil throws on your ways to defeat us can be converted to stepping-stones for victory. If you carefully go through the Bible, it will be clear that great problems always precede great triumphs. Goliath was pain in the neck of Israel, but David was never promoted until he killed Goliath. The troubles which David faced was a stepping stone to fame and popularity. David challenged Goliath. He brought his head down by the power of the Lord and great victory was wrought on that day.

If David refused challenges, he would have remained at the lowest rung of the ladder. He would not have received the shouts of praise or encomium showered on him. David became a great man because he passed through great problems. If there is any Goliath in your way now, the Goliath will become the stepping-stone to your promotion. Every Goliath has an unprotected forehead, which the stone of your prayer can locate.

When you want uncommon breakthroughs or you want to be an uncommon person then go ahead and solve an uncommon problem. Defeat an uncommon enemy like Goliath.

Great problems often precede great triumphs and great victories. In God's mathematics, it is not possible to get to the Promised Land without passing through the wilderness. God's people are not without problems. The great consolation is that God is with them in problem. Consider what the book of Isaiah says:

Isaiah 43:2 - When thou passest through the waters, I will be with thee; and through the rivers, they shall not overflow thee: when thou walkest through the fire, thou shalt not be burned; neither shall the flame kindle upon thee

Note the word, "when". It does not say "if". "When" implies that a time will definitely come when you will pass through difficulties. Problems provide a platform through which the Lord displays His power, love and mercy.

NO BATTLE, NO VICTORY

Every irritation the enemy brings across your way is really an invitation to elevation, especially if you are a true child of God. Most of the wells of joy that were dug in the Bible, were dug by God with the spade of sorrow. God will not deliver you from your problems but he will deliver you in spites of the problems. He said that all the enemies who come against you should flee before your face. If they come against you in one way they shall flee in seven ways. But remember that they will surely come against you.

When we were still young in the ministry, an old pastor was invited to talk to us. The man said that he had no lecture for us but that he had two questions:

Question number one: Why is it that we do not see people stoning preachers these days as it was done unto Stephen? One man said, "Daddy, it is because there is civilization". Another person said, "Daddy, people will arrest whosoever stones a preacher". Somebody said, "It is because demons have devised another method. The demons will not be involved in throwing stones but they will send beautiful ladies to seduce you so that you might fall". The old pastor condemned every answer given.

After we had exhausted all our answers, the man looked at us and said "The reason preachers are not stoned today is because the stone throwers do not know who to stone". He continue, "The day you get to the level of the spirituality of Stephen they would stone you".

The old man then asked the second question: He brought out his second question form the hymn book. The hymn read ... "There is victory in my soul. Victory ahead, victory ahead". The old man then asked, "How many of you wants to be victorious over all problems"? Everybody put up his hands. He said, "Anybody who wants the greatest victory, shout halleluiah!" He said, "How many of you want problems"? We all kept quiet. He then commented, "You want victory but you do not want problems. How then will you experience victory?"

Many are crying day and night when they should not cry at all. Many have allowed the enemy to discourage their hearts. Many take the words of medical doctors as the final verdict. Many base their lives on "expert" opinion. Such people's troubles will escalate. I knew a man who was suffering from asthma. We went to his home. I entered his library and discovered that it was filled with books on asthma. I then asked him, "Sir, why do you have several volumes on asthma?" He said, "Since I have asthma, I want to read more about it". Reading about a problem does not solve the problem.

The truth about life is that, you are your best when faced with great opposition. You cannot run away from battles and expect victory. Every problem has its opportunities. Most of the things we call problems are God's instruments to fashion us into his model. What you call problems may be God's servants to make you become the best you can be. If a problem is coming upon you, it is an indication that your life is a threat to some powers. If you have no problem and you have no enemy then you must be sure that you are finished. It means heaven has forgotten you and the devil, too, has written you off. It means the devil has given you a red card to depart from the field of play. It means you are no longer a victim of his attacks. The devil wages wars against those he considers very risky to his kingdom.

THE ANTIDOTE

When all the money is gone, what do you do? When you are indebted, what do you do? What do you do when your life is upside down and the unbelievers are laughing at you? What do you do when members of your family gather around you and say, "Well, we have decide to invite you to this meeting so that we can deliberate about your life? What will you do when they start to compare you with your mates, and with your younger brothers and sisters who have gotten married and are doing fine? What do you do when your family members conclude that your case is the worst and that you require fetish doctors to wash your head? What do you do when people mock your saviour that he cannot deliver you?

LESSONS TO BE LEARNT WHEN YOU ARE AT YOUR WITS' END

1. **God has the ability and the capacity to provide an authentic solution to any problem:** When there seems to be no way, stop running around. Stop wasting your time. Stop moving around from one family member to another. If things improve, they will look for you. Stop going to beggarly places. God has not traveled anywhere. He can provide an alternative solution to any problem where there seems to be no way. Do you believe this?

2. **God can make a way when humanly speaking, there is no way and all hopes are blocked:** That is why the Bible says that God can bing honey out of the rock. He can order the rock to bring out honey. If you jump ahead because of the spirit of discouragement and despair, you will be killed by the enemy in no distant time.

3. **God is not limited to one method of operation:** Our problem, most of the time is that, we focus on only one direction. We are yet to learn that God's ways cannot be predicted. Some are waiting for God at the backyard when He is coming through the window. If I pray that before you are through with reading this book you will become a millionaire, I am sure your response would be an overwhelming Amen. But, you might be entertaining doubt saying, "How can this be possible? How can I become a millionaire so soon? That is how many people limit God.

ACCORDING TO YOUR FAITH

I have a friend whose faith was a challenge to me when I was a young Christian. His faith was so strange and strong that he never bought insecticides to kill mosquitoes. He would lie on the bed and say: "Lord, your servant is going to bed now. Your words say: He gives his beloved sleep. Therefore, you mosquitoes, hear the word of the Lord; My body is not your food. I silence your mouth, in the name of Jesus, Amen". He would then sleep off. Although, the mosquitoes would be singing in his ears but they would not move near him. That was how he continued until the day he got married.

When he got home after the wedding. At night mosquitoes continued to hover around the room. The wife said, "Where is an insecticide to kill these mosquitoes". The brother said, "I do not use insecticides against mosquitoes.

I only talk to them". The wife said, "You! Talk to mosquitoes? Nonsense! Let us go and buy insecticides. Why should you be so stingy?" That night he prayed as he used to but mosquitoes dealt with both of them. The wall had broken down.

This friend of mine woke up one day and said, "God told me that I am going to America. He had visa but no ticket. He said, "I am traveling to America tomorrow". He was asked, "What about the ticket?". "I don't have a ticket" was the answer. Do you know that he got to the airport without a ticket? He queued up to be checked in. He gave them his passport and they asked him, "What of the ticket?" He said, "I don't have. But the Lord said, He would take me to America". The woman who was checking them in said, "Sir, do not trouble me, step aside".

There was a white man who was standing behind the brother and heard all the discussions. The white man was challenged when the brother said "The Lord will take me there". The white man volunteered saying, "I will pay". Indeed, God cannot be limited. The brother traveled to America through persistent faith.

THE SAME PROBLEM, DIFFERENT SOLUTIONS

Let us take the example of our Lord Jesus to establish the fact that God cannot be limited. Jesus Christ ministered to those who had the problem of blindness in at least five different ways. In the same vein, life's problems come in five different ways.

i. A blind man came to Jesus and Jesus **touched** him and he saw.
ii. Jesus **spat** on the floor and applied it to the eyes of another blind man and his eyes got opened.
iii. Jesus **bound** the spirit of blindness and a particular blind man saw
iv. Jesus **spoke** the word and another blind man saw
v. **Ordinary Jesus** made **clay** and applied on another blind man and his eyes got opened.

It was as if the man left heaven in a hurry and forgot his eyeballs. Jesus made clay and put it in the place of the eyes and the man could see. They had the same problem but got different solutions.

If you have a negative mind-set about your problem, then you have missed it. I counsel you to allow God to operate the way He wants in your case.

4. **Causes of problems differ:** The depth and the seriousness if problems also differ. That is why you should not compare yourself with any one. This is why Jesus ministered to a blind man twice. Jesus, whose faith was perfect and absolute, had to minister to him twice.

5. **There is a spiritual force behind every problem.**
 In one of our crusades in America, a white lady was brought in. She spoke to me and said that her great great grandmother died of breast cancer, her great grand mother died of breast cancer, her grandmother also died of breast cancer. Her mother died of breast cancer, too.

She did not want to die of breast cancer, she decided to cut off her two breasts.

Although there was no sign or symptom nor diagnosis of cancer of the breast, she cut them off. Her view was that wince the cancer attacks breasts, if there was no breast then cancer would not come. "There is no breast for cancer to attack" she thought. But, strange enough, the cancer attacked her liver.

Problems differ. The depth of problems also differ. There is an unseen spiritual force behind problems. When the spiritual force attacked the white lady and there was no breast, it located another organ in the body. My prayer is that every organised enemy against you shall be scattered in Jesus name.

6. **Launch a violent counter attack on satanic operation in your life:** You must do so when you notice that you have no place to go as all the roads around you are blocked.

7. **Cry out and God will intervene:** The last lesson shall be picked from Psalms 107:26-30

Ps. 107:26-30: They mount up to the heaven, they go down again to the depths: their soul is melted because of trouble. They reel to and fro, and stagger like a drunken man, and are at their wits' end. Then they cry unto the LORD in their trouble, and he bringeth them out of their distresses. He maketh the storm a calm, so that the waves thereof are still. Then are they glad because they be quiet; so he bringeth them unto their desired haven.

Cry unto the God of Elijah. Elijah himself cried unto the God of Abraham, Isaac and Jacob. When it got to the turn of Elisha, he cried unto the God of Elijah. When you cry as Elisha did at river Jordan, :Where is the Lord God of Elijah?" Something must happen because the God of Elijah answered immediately. Whatever Elisha did at the other side of Jordan worked. When you at your wits' end cry unto the God of Elijah and He will answer.

Elijah was harassed by Jezebel. Elijah was about to leave a difficult job for Elisha. Elisha knew that a single portion of Elijah's power would not do the job effectively. Elisha was already on the other side of Jordan. Elisha could do nothing as man's intelligence was useless to him. Wild animals would have killed him there. He then cried out "Where is the Lord God of Elijah? Then God answered.

When you are at your wits' end and you cry unto the Lord God of Elijah, things will always happen. It is time to challenge all your enemies as Elijah did to all prophets of Ball. Fear and difficulties may pile up as mountains, they would crumble as you cry unto the God of Elijah.

Are there powers preventing you from your breakthroughs? Are demons trying to prevent you from entering the promised land? Are evil powers planning for your demotion when God is calling you for promotion? Are they polluting your potentials? Are they serving as barriers to your promotion?

Has the enemies trapped your children, wife or husband in a strange land? If you will cry unto the God of Elijah, salvation will come from the Lord.

Any power militating against the power of Elijah is planning to sink into the Red Sea after the order of Pharaoh. Such a power is planning to be destroyed by the angels which destroyed Sennacherib.

Any power that is militating against a child of God is looking for real trouble. The trouble seeker will eventually receive compulsory burial. Any power that is opposing your life is writing a letter to trouble and commotion. It is seeking to be eaten up after the order of Herod.

The power of the enemy might have forgotten that the Lord is a man of war. He is a mighty and terrible warrior. Read what the Bible says:

Job 9:4 : He is wise in heart, and mighty in strength: who hath hardened himself against him, and hath prospered?

If the Lord should raise one finger, all the hosts of heaven will begin to fight. The sun, the moon and stars will wage war on such a soul. Today, God will arise on your behalf and He will harass your enemies, in the name of Jesus.

PRAYER POINTS

1. Any power of my father's house that wants me to die in abject poverty, die, in the name of Jesus.

2. In the presence of every power that is asking, "Where is my God" Oh God of Elijah manifest your power, in the name of Jesus.

3. Where is the God of Elijah? Arise and let problem die, in the name of Jesus.

4. Any power that does not want to let me go when God says, "Go", die, in the name of Jesus.

5. Any power assigned to frustrate me, what are you waiting for? die, in the name of Jesus.

6. Goliath that stands against my destiny, hear the word of the Lord, die, in the name of Jesus.

7. Any local power behind my problem, die, in the name of Jesus.

When The Enemy Is At Large

Life does not tolerate a vacuum. When you are not in charge, then someone else would be. When God is never allowed to reign, Satan will take up the saddle of leadership.

This message is a prophetic message and not a scientific one. Prophesy and science are two parallel lines. This is not to say that scientists do not know God. One thing is sure, God can never be subjected to scientific experiments. He cannot be infused into the tube for testing, observation and inference.

When the strongman is at large and there is no man to tame or arrest him, what do we experience in such a situation? This is the focus of this message.

There are two scriptural references to be examined.

The first is in Daniel 10:1-3

Daniel 10: 1-3: In the third year of Cyrus king of Persia a thing was revealed unto Daniel, whose name was called Belteshazzar; and the thing was true, but the time appointed was long: and he understood the thing, and had understanding of the vision. In those days I Daniel was mourning three full weeks. I ate no pleasant bread, neither came flesh nor wine in my mouth, neither did I anoint myself at all, till three whole weeks were fulfilled.

Daniel prayed for twenty one days not for himself but for his nation. He prayed hard in those days but the answer did not come. He was bothered like any of us will be when answers to our prayers are delayed.

of Jesus Christ had made you to crash-land, will you give your life of Jesus? She blurted, "No, I have sold my soul to the devil!". This proves that every nation, locality or institution has powers of darkness waging war against it.

UNDERSTANDING LOCAL STRONGMAN

The enemy has an agenda which bothers on wasting young people. That is why teachers, parents and lecturers who teach young people are always objects of attack.

The next reference that needs consideration is in the book of Matthew.

Matt, 12:29: Or else how can one enter into a strong man's house, and spoil his goods, except he first bind the strong man? and then he will spoil his house.

Jesus identify a personality called the strongman. Let us gain further insight into the understanding of who the strongman is from Luke's gospel.

Luke 11:21: When a strong man armed keepeth his palace, his goods are in peace:

This is a personality called the strongman. He has what the Bible refers to as his goods. The strongman remains in control until a stronger power comes upon him.

There are different powers in charge of different localities. The way they operate varies from one locality to another. The strongman of a particular community is the controller of the environment. He is a representative of the devil because the devil is not omnipresent. He, therefore, needs representatives to take care of his interests.

A strongman is the principal force or the evil power controlling a particular place. The strongman believes that his environment was handed over to him and so he could manipulate the environment the way he wants. The strongman is a king who resides in the palace of darkness in a particular location. Every city, family, institution has its own invisible strongman. If a problem keeps staring at you in the face in such a way that it refuses to go after much prayers, then a strongman is in charge of such a problem. The problem would persist until the strongman is arrested or disgraced.

The strongman is a commander-in-chief of the dark kingdom assigned to a particular place. When the strongman is in charge, it will invite other wicked spirits.

WHEN THE ENEMY IS AT LARGE

A strongman can be wicked when he is at large. All kinds of things happen when the enemy is at large. When this happens, there will be disaster, chaos, violence and bloodshed. Why? It is because these evil occurrences are the fertilizers for the strongman to feed on.

There is a personal strongman, a family strongman and an institutional strongman. When the strongman is at large, confusion and commotion will take place.

The strongman could be attached to career or business. It could be attached to a person's marriage. It could also be attached to academics. And once they break loose in any area, tragedy and loss of lives would occur. When the strongman is in charge, life becomes unbearable. When the strongman is at large, there will be chains of problems. When one problem goes, another one will come. Terrible dreams, nightmares are the kinds of things that happen to people who are supervised by a strongman who can not be located.

There are powers that could be found in the locality where the strongman controls. To deal with any strongman, there is a need for spiritual mapping of the place in order to identify and ascertain the powers that are prevalent. Here are some of the powers that could be dominant in a particular locality.

1. Marine powers - This prevails where there is proximity to a river or water. People in riverrine areas suffer a lot from this power. To worsen the situation, evil names may be given to the rivers.
2. Delegated agents
3. Occult practitioners - Fetish workers or fetish boys and girls abound both in civilized and primitive societies.
4. Original inhabitants of the land
5. Drinkers of blood and eaters of flesh
6. Demonic caterers - Those who are selling polluted food.

7. Spirit of sexual perversion
8. Spirit that twist the mind and bend logic
9. Religious spirits
10. International demons
11. Destiny "quenchers" who are called wasters
12. Spirit of pride
13. Spirit of deception
14. Spirit of violence
15. Spirit of destruction
16. Spirit of spiritual coldness
17. Spirit of untimely death
18. Spirit of rebellion - rebellion goes beyond youthful exuberance, there is personality behind it.
19. Familiar spirit - This spirit operates among both young and old people who, at the slightest provocation, cause havocs.
20. Modern witchcraft - These are the present day witchcraft operation. Those forms of witchcraft use the latest perfume. Most of them are very young people and they cause all kinds of havoc.

Recently, I was in Europe and I had the privilege of being among those allowed to visit their prison in order to minister. I obtained the form as a preacher who came in to preach to the prisoners. As I was signing the form, a young man also came in. He wore a black shirt, a black suit, a black wrist watch, a pair of black sandal; everything on him was black including spectacles. He introduced himself saying, "I am a witch. I have come to speak to the prisoners!" He was hiding under freedom of speech and religion.

The tragedy of the incident was that when we all got in to minister to the prisoners the wizard had a larger audience then the minister of the gospel. Indeed, we are up in arms against an enemy who is at large!

WHAT TO DO
1. Repent - Repent on your behalf and on behalf of others for all evils committed against God and against humanity

2. Address the spiritual strongman

PRAYER POINTS
1. Oh God, arise and let the powers that are gathered against my life and family, scatter, in the name of Jesus.

2. Every serpent and scorpion assigned against me, scatter, in the name of Jesus.

3. Every occult power, operating in my locality, die, in the name of Jesus.

4. Every agent of darkness, operating in my family, loose your power, in the name of Jesus.

5. Every strongman assigned against me, your time is up, die, in the name of Jesus.

6. Altar of satanic exchange in my family life, die, in the name of Jesus.

7. Any power, that wants to attack me, bow down and die, in the name of Jesus.

8. Every witchcraft power drinking the blood of Nigerians, die, in the name of Jesus.

9. Every arrow of wickedness, targeted against my destiny, die, in the name of Jesus.

10. Every Goliath of impossibility, die, in the name of Jesus.

11. Wherever the enemy has knocked me down, my Father, raise me up, in the name of Jesus.

12. Every owner of the load of infirmity, carry your load by fire, in the name of Jesus.

13. I claim divine rearrangement for supernatural living, in the name of Jesus.

14. I claim divine re-arrangement for restoration, outstanding miracles, break through, supernatural anointing, in the name of Jesus.

15. God of Daniel empower me for unchallengeable victory, in the name of Jesus.

16. I reject the armour of Saul and I receive the stone of fire to destroy my Goliath, in the name of Jesus.

17. My Goliath, enter your grave forever, in Jesus' name.

18. Every arrow of witchcraft power, against my future, backfire by fire, in the name of Jesus.
19. Every satanic battle at the point of my harvest, die, in the name of Jesus.
20. Every decree of death, over my life, be revoked by fire, in the name of Jesus.
21. Every dream of death, accident and tragedy be reversed, by the blood of Jesus, in the name of Jesus.
22. I shall not die but live to declare the wonderful works of God, in the name of Jesus.
23. Every satanic traffic warder, diverting my blessings, die by fire, in the name of Jesus.
24. After the order of dry-bones let all my fragmented benefit come back to me, in the name of Jesus.
25. God of perfection, perfect everything that concerns my life, in the name of Jesus.
26. Every evil pot, cooking my glory, die, in Jesus' name.
27. Generational curses, die by the blood of Jesus, in the name of Jesus.
28. Where is the Lord God of Elijah? Arise and use all your weapons to disgrace my enemies, in the name of Jesus.
29. Every Pharaoh pursuing my Moses, die, in Jesus' name.
30. Umbrella of fire, protect me and my family throughout this year, in the name of Jesus.

31. Wherever my name is being mentioned for untimely death, Rock of Ages, grind them to powder, in Jesus' name.

32. Thou power of slow death, die, in the name of Jesus.

33. Hammer of fire, break the coffin of darkness, in the name of Jesus.

34. "I am that I am", arise, manifest your power in my life, in the name of Jesus.

35. Every evil power, struggling to restructure my destiny, die, in the name of Jesus.

36. God of Elijah, unseat, move and transfer anybody blocking my promotion, in the name of Jesus.

37. Every blessing, stolen from me in the 12 months of this year, I repossess you, in the name of Jesus.

38. Where is the Lord God of Elijah? Arise make me an example of what Your power can do, in Jesus' name.

39. My destiny, awake and put on the strength of God, in the name of Jesus.

40. Oh God arise and give me ease of accomplishment, in the name of Jesus.

41. Every power that is attacking the will of my destiny, die, in the name of Jesus.

42. Favour, my life is available for you, enter, in the name of Jesus.

43. Spiritual waster, release my finances, in Jesus' name.
44. Spiritual waster, release my life, in the name of Jesus.
45. Every authority, dominion of household witchcraft, die, in the name of Jesus.
46. Every Pharaoh, release me, in the name of Jesus.
47. Household witchcraft, carry your load in my life by fire, in the name of Jesus.
48. Spirit of the Dead Sea in my life, I hate you, die, in the name of Jesus.
49. I break all the chains of stagnancy, in my life, in the name of Jesus.
50. I receive the anointing to move forward by fire, in the name of Jesus.
51. Every embargo upon my life, die, in the name of Jesus.
52. Every power, assigned to frustrate me, die, in the name of Jesus.
53. Where is the job that will bless my life? Come to me now, in the name of Jesus.
54. Every seed of aimlessness, that is growing with my destiny, die by fire, in the name of Jesus.
55. Every foundation of aimlessness laid by my ancestors for my destiny, be dismantled by fire, in Jesus' name.
56. My destiny, refuse to be wasted, in the name of Jesus.

57. Every power, that is watching my day of glory in my father's house, in order to disgrace me, I pull you down, in the name of Jesus.

58. Every tree of non achievement that has been trailing my destiny, I cut you off, in the name of Jesus.

59. I receive power for divine focus, in the name of Jesus.

60. I receive power to pursue my career to fulfillment, in the name of Jesus.

61. Spirit of excellence fall upon me now, in Jesus' name.

62. Every spirit of the wasters and devourers, promoting poverty in my life, die, in the name of Jesus.

63. You my legs, refuse to walk into poverty, my hands refuse to take the gift of poverty, therefore, every attachment to poverty in my life, die, in Jesus' name.

64. My Father, give me the miracle that will swallow poverty in my life, in the name of Jesus.

65. I purge my life and my destiny, from profitless hard work by the blood of Jesus, in the name of Jesus.

66. I break and loose my life from profitless hard work, in the name of Jesus.

67. Every cloth of profitless hard work in my destiny, I tear it off by fire, in the name of Jesus.

68. Every mark of shame and disgrace in my destiny, be wiped off by the blood of Jesus.

69. Every instrument of disgrace, fashioned against my life backfire, in the name of Jesus.

70. Any power, planning to disgrace my life wherever you are now, die, in the name of Jesus.

71. Satanic marital covenant, break, in the name of Jesus.

72. Every dream of the past, that is now affecting my future, die, in the name of Jesus.

73. Babylon wall of unemployment, distress, stagnancy, fall and rise no more, in the name of Jesus.

74. Oh hand of break-through, leave heaven for my sake, in the name of Jesus.

75. Oh hand of fire, leave heaven and fight for me, in the name of Jesus.

76. Oh Babylon wall of failure, fall and rise no more, in the name of Jesus.

77. Every Babylon wall of household witchcraft, fall and rise no more, in the name of Jesus.

78. Babylon wall of failure at the edge of success fall and rise no more, in the name of Jesus.

79. Oh hand from heaven, arise write the obituary of my problems by fire, in the name of Jesus.

80. Every satanic equation for my life, change by fire, in the name of Jesus.

81. Every satanic agenda for my life, in this month, die, in the name of Jesus.

82. Every voice crying to the heavenlies to waste my destiny, be wiped off, in the name of Jesus.

83. Every negative anointing, speaking against me, die, in the name of Jesus.

84. Every witchcraft vision, programmed into my dream, die, in the name of Jesus.

85. Stubborn strongman, release the key of my breakthroughs, in the name of Jesus.

86. I break the confidence of darkness, in Jesus' name.

87. I declare to the heavens that my life shall not be wasted, in the name of Jesus.

88. Every power, that swallows opportunities, be wasted, in the name of Jesus.

89. Every power, that swallows virtue, be wasted, in the name of Jesus.

90. Every power, that swallows resources, be wasted, in the name of Jesus.

91. Every stubborn witchcraft power, be wasted, in the name of Jesus.

92. Every career waster, be wasted, in the name of Jesus.

93. Every marriage waster, be wasted, in Jesus' name.

94. Every destiny waster, be wasted, in the name of Jesus.

95. Every altar of witchcraft, designed against me, be wasted now, in the name of Jesus.

96. Every power, attacking my finances be wasted, in the name of Jesus.

97. Any power, that does not want me to rise and shine, waste, in the name of Jesus.

98. Every ancient family decree, working against my full testimony, be wasted, in the name of Jesus.

99. Every power, speaking frustration into my life, be wasted, in the name of Jesus.

100. Every power, rising against my deliverance, waste, in the name of Jesus.

101. Any power, that want to waste my life, waste by fire, in the name of Jesus.

102. Oh God arise, and let every waster, be wasted, in the name of Jesus.

103. Every placenta bondage, that wants to waste my life, be wasted, in the name of Jesus.

104. Every power of familiar spirit of my father's house, that wants to waste my life be wasted by fire, in the name of Jesus.

105. Beginning from this month, my miracle shall overflow, in the name of Jesus.

106. Oh heavens, harken to my voice and fight for me, in the name of Jesus.

107. Let all my prayerful requests become powerful testimonies, in the name of Jesus.

108. I fire back, every arrow of death, in the name of Jesus.

109. Every dream oppressor, die, in the name of Jesus.

110. Every evil horn, scattering my break-through, carpenter of God, kill them, in the name of Jesus.

111. Where is the Lord God of Elijah, arise and recover my glory, in the name of Jesus.

112. Thou power of darkness, challenging my destiny, I bury you today, in the name of Jesus.

113. Every witchcraft arrow, fired into my life, as a baby, come out and go back to your sender, in Jesus' name.

114. Oh horns of darkness, I throw you into the wall of fire, in the name of Jesus.

115. Plantation of darkness in my destiny, die, in the name of Jesus.

116. In the presence of those asking for my God this year, Oh God arise, manifest your power, in Jesus' name.

117. Every power of blood shed, in my community, die, in the name of Jesus.

118. Oh star of my life, do not sit down, arise, shine, in the name of Jesus.

119. Every tragedy in this month, minus me and my family, in the name of Jesus.

120. Oh God arise and let my problems die, in Jesus' name.

121. Oh God arise and let my Pharaoh die, in Jesus' name.

122. Oh God arise and let my Goliath die, in Jesus' name.

123. Oh God arise and let my stubborn pursuers scatter, in the name of Jesus.

124. Oh God arise and manifest your power in my life, in the name of Jesus.

125. Oh God arise and promote me by fire, in Jesus' name.

126. Oh God arise and let my breakthroughs manifest, in the name of Jesus.

127. Uncommon breakthroughs arise locate me, in the name of Jesus.

128. My Father, catapult me seven time faster to my next level in life, in the name of Jesus.

129. Every power, bearing my name in demonic world, die, in the name of Jesus.

130. Blood of Jesus, roar like a thunder and pursue my pursuer, in the name of Jesus.

131. My Jordan, disappear, my Jericho wall, scatter, in the name of Jesus.

132. Every yoke of infirmity, break, in the name of Jesus.

133. Every curse of backwardness, be broken, in the name of Jesus.

134. Every village witchcraft, contesting for my destiny, die, in the name of Jesus.

135. Every evil pronouncement, uttered against me, be condemned, in the name of Jesus.

136. Anointing of possibilities, come upon me, in the name of Jesus.

137. Foundational curses, limiting my breakthroughs, die by the blood of Jesus, in the name of Jesus.

138. Every owner of tragedy and sorrow, carry your load by fire, in the name of Jesus.

139. Spirit of breakthroughs and favour, overshadow my life, in the name of Jesus.

140. Every satanic agenda for Nigeria, we bury you today, in the name of Jesus.

141. Thou glory of Nigeria, arise by fire and shine, in the name of Jesus.

142. Blood of Jesus, arise in your power, deliver my foundation, in the name of Jesus.

143. Every rope of darkness, connecting me to any dead relative, break, in the name of Jesus.

144. Harvest of iniquity of my father's house, die by the blood of Jesus, in the name of Jesus.

145. Harvest of iniquity of my mother's house, die by the blood of Jesus, in the name of Jesus.

146. Foundational poverty, die, in the name of Jesus.

147. Foundational witchcraft, die, in the name of Jesus.

148. Foundation of backwardness in my life, die, in the name of Jesus.

149. Every witchcraft power, delegated against my progress, die, in the name of Jesus.

150. Every arrow of failure, backfire, in the name of Jesus.

151. Where is the Lord God of Elijah, arise by fire, pursue my pursuer, in the name of Jesus.

152. Every altar of satan in my family, die, in the name of Jesus.

153. Every territorial bondage, walking against my destiny, die, in the name of Jesus.

154. Every foundational power, summoning me to the bottom, scatter, in the name of Jesus.

155. Every serpent and scorpion of frustration, die, in the name of Jesus.

156. Yoke of my family shrine, be broken, in the name of Jesus. (Amen).

Other Publications by Dr. D. K. Olukoya, published and marketed by The Battle Cry Christian Ministries

1. 20 Marching Orders To Fulfill Your Destiny
2. 30 Things The Anointing Can Do For You
3. A-Z of Complete Deliverance
4. Abraham's Children in Bondage
5. Be Prepared
6. Bewitchment must die
7. Biblical Principles of Dream Interpretation
8. Born Great, But Tied Down
9. Breaking Bad Habits
10. Breakthrough Prayers For Business Professionals
11. Brokenness
12. Bringing Down The Power of God
13. Can God?
14. Can God Trust You?
15. Command The Morning
16. Consecration Commitment & Loyalty
17. Contending For The Kingdom
18. Connecting to The God of Breakthroughs
19. Criminals In The House Of God
20. Dancers At The Gate of Death
21. Dealing With Hidden Curses
22. Dealing With Local Satanic Technology
23. Dealing With Satanic Exchange
24. Dealing With The Evil Powers Of Your Father's House
25. Dealing With Tropical Demons
26. Dealing With Unprofitable Roots
27. Dealing With Witchcraft Barbers
28. Deliverance By Fire
29. Deliverance From Spirit Husband And Spirit Wife
30. Deliverance From The Limiting Powers

Other Publications by Dr. D. K. Olukoya, published and marketed by The Battle Cry Christian Ministries

31. Deliverance of The Brain
32. Deliverance Of The Conscience
33. Deliverance Of The Head
34. Deliverance of The Tongue
35. Deliverance: God's Medicine Bottle
36. Destiny Clinic
37. Destroying Satanic Masks
38. Disgracing Soul Hunters
39. Divine Military Training
40. Divine Yellow Card
41. Dominion Prosperity
42. Drawers Of Power From The Heavenlies
43. Evil Appetite
44. Evil Umbrella
45. Facing Both Ways
46. Failure In The School Of Prayer
47. Fire For Life's Journey
48. For We Wrestle ...
49. Freedom Indeed
50. God's Key To A Happy Life
51. Holiness Unto The Lord
52. Holy Cry
53. Holy Fever
54. Hour Of Decision
55. How To Obtain Personal Deliverance
56. How To Pray When Surrounded By The Enemies
57. Idols Of The Heart
58. Is This What They Died For?
59. Killing The Serpent of Frustration
60. Let God Answer By Fire

Other Publications by Dr. D. K. Olukoya, published and marketed by The Battle Cry Christian Ministries

61. Lord, Behold Their Threatening
62. Limiting God
63. Madness Of The Heart
64. Making Your Way Through The Traffic Jam of Life
65. Meat For Champions
66. Medicine For Winners
67. My Burden For The Church
68. Open Heavens Through Holy Disturbance
69. Overpowering Witchcraft
70. Paralysing The Riders And The Horse
71. Personal Spiritual Check-Up
72. Principles of Conclusive Prayers
73. Possessing The Tongue of Fire
74. Power Against Coffin Spirits
75. Power Against Destiny Quenchers
76. Power Against Dream Criminals
77. Power Against Local Wickedness
78. Power Against Marine Spirits
79. Power Against Spiritual Terrorists
80. Power To Recover Your Lost Glory
81. Power Must Change Hands
82. Pray Your Way To Breakthroughs
83. Prayer Is The Battle
84. Prayer Rain
85. Prayer Strategies For Spinsters And Bachelors
86. Prayer To Kill Enchantment
87. Prayer To Make You Fulfill Your Divine Destiny
88. Prayer Warfare Against 70 Mad Spirits
89. Prayers For Open Heavens
90. Prayers To Destroy Diseases And Infirmities

Other Publications by Dr. D. K. Olukoya, published and marketed by The Battle Cry Christian Ministries

91. Prayers To Move From Minimum To Maximum
92. Praying Against The Spirit Of The Valley
93. Praying To Destroy Satanic Roadblocks
94. Praying To Dismantle Witchcraft
95. Principles Of Prayer
96. Release From Destructive Covenants
97. Revoking Evil Decrees
98. Safeguarding Your Home
99. Satanic Diversion Of The Black Race
100. Setting The Covens Ablaze
101. Seventy Sermons To Preach To Your Destiny
102. Silencing The Birds Of Darkness
103. Slaves Who Love Their Chains
104. Smite The Enemy And He Will Flee
105. Speaking Destruction Unto The Dark Rivers
106. Spiritual Education
107. Spiritual Growth And Maturity
108. Spiritual Warfare And The Home
109. Strategic Praying
110. Strategy Of Warfare Praying
111. Stop Them Before They Stop You
112. Students In The School Of Fear
113. Symptoms Of Witchcraft Attack
114. The Baptism of Fire
115. The Battle Against The Spirit Of Impossibility
116. The Dinning Table Of Darkness
117. The Enemy Has Done This
118. The Evil Cry Of Your Family Idol
119. The Fire Of Revival
120. The Great Deliverance

Other Publications by Dr. D. K. Olukoya, published and marketed by The Battle Cry Christian Ministries

121. The Internal Stumbling Block
122. The Lord Is A Man Of War
123. The Mystery Of Mobile Curses
124. The Mystery Of The Mobile Temple
125. The Prayer Eagle
126. The Power of Aggressive Prayer Warriors
127. The Power of Priority
128. The Pursuit Of Success
129. The Seasons Of Life
130. The Secrets Of Greatness
131. The Serpentine Enemies
132. The Skeleton In Your Grandfather's Cupboard
133. The Slow Learners
134. The Snake In The Power House
135. The Spirit Of The Crab
136. The star hunters
137. The Star In Your Sky
138. The Terrible Agenda
139. The Tongue Trap
140. The Unconquerable Power
141. The Unlimited God
142. The Vagabond Spirit
143. The Way Of Divine Encounter
144. The Wealth Transfer Agenda
145. Tied Down In The Spirits
146. Too Hot To Handle
147. Turnaround Breakthrough
148. Unprofitable Foundations
149. Victory Over Satanic Dreams
150. Victory Over Your Greatest Enemies

Other Publications by Dr. D. K. Olukoya, published and marketed by The Battle Cry Christian Ministries

151. Violent Prayers Against Stubborn Situations
152. War At The Edge Of Breakthroughs
153. Wasting The Wasters
154. Wasted At The Market Square of Life
155. Wealth Must Change Hands
156. What You Must Know About The House Fellowship
157. When God Is Silent
158. When the Battle is from Home
159. When The Deliverer Need Deliverance
160. When Things Get Hard
161. When You Are Knocked Down
162. Where Is Your Faith
163. While Men Slept
164. Woman! Thou Art Loosed.
165. Your Battle And Your Strategy
166. Your Foundation And Destiny
167. Your Mouth And Your Deliverance

YORUBA PUBLICATIONS
1. ADURA AGBAYORI
2. ADURA TI NSI OKE NIDI
3. OJO ADURA

FRENCH PUBLICATIONS
1. PLUIE DE PRIERE
2. ESPIRIT DE VAGABONDAGE
3. EN FINIR AVEC LES FORCES MALEFIQUES DE LA MAISON DE TON PERE
4. QUE I'ENVOUTEMENT PERISSE
5. FRAPPEZ I'ADVERSAIRE ET IL FUIRA
6. COMMENT RECEVIOR LA DELIVRANCE DU MARI ET FEMME DE NUIT

Other Publications by Dr. D. K. Olukoya, published and marketed by The Battle Cry Christian Ministries

7. CPMMENT SE DELIVRER SOI-MEME
8. POVOIR CONTRE LES TERRORITES SPIRITUEL
9. PRIERE DE PERCEES POUR LES HOMMES D'AFFAIRES
10. PRIER JUSQU'A REMPORTER LA VICTOIRE
11. PRIERES VIOLENTES POUR HUMILIER LES PROBLEMES OPINIATRES
12. PRIERE POUR DETRUIRE LES MALADIES ET INFIRMITES
13. LE COMBAT SPIRITUEL ET LE FOYER
14. BILAN SPIRITUEL PERSONNEL
15. VICTOIRES SUR LES REVES SATANIQUES
16. PRIERES DE COMAT CONTRE 70 ESPIRITS DECHANINES
17. LA DEVIATION SATANIQUE DE LA RACE NOIRE
18. TON COMBAT ET TA STRATEGIE
19. VOTRE FONDEMENT ET VOTRE DESTIN
20. REVOQUER LES DECRETS MALEFIQUES
21. CANTIQUE DES CONTIQUES
22. LE MAUVAIS CRI DES IDOLES
23. QUAND LES CHOSES DEVIENNENT DIFFICILES
24. LES STRATEGIES DE PRIERES POUR LES CELIBATAIRES
25. SE LIBERER DES ALLIANCES MALEFIQUES
26. DEMANTELER LA SORCELLERIE
27. LA DELIVERANCE: LE FLACON DE MEDICAMENT DIEU
28. LA DELIVERANCE DE LA TETE
29. COMMANDER LE MATIN
30. NE GRAND MAIS LIE
31. POUVOIR CONTRE LES DEMOND TROPICAUX
32. LE PROGRAMME DE TRANFERT DE RICHESSE
33. LES ETUDIANTS A I'ECOLE DE LA PEUR
34. L'ETOILE DANS VOTRE CIEL
35. LES SAISONS DE LA VIE
36. FEMME TU ES LIBEREE

**Other Publications by Dr. D. K. Olukoya, published
and marketed by The Battle Cry Christian Ministries**

ANNUAL 70 DAYS PRAYER AND FASTING PUBLICATIONS

1. Prayers That Bring Miracles
2. Let God Answer By Fire
3. Prayers To Mount With Wings As Eagles
4. Prayers That Bring Explosive Increase
5. Prayers For Open Heavens
6. Prayers To Make You Fulfill Your Divine Destiny
7. Prayers That Make God To Answer And Fight By Fire
8. Prayers That Bring Unchallengeable Victory And Breakthrough Rainfall Bombardments
9. Prayers That Bring Dominion Prosperity And Uncommon Success
10. Prayers That Bring Power And Overflowing Progress
11. Prayers That Bring Laughter And Enlargement Breakthroughs
12. Prayers That Bring Uncommon Favour And Breakthroughs
13. Prayers That Bring Unprecedented Greatness & Unmatchable Increase
14. Prayers That Bring Awesome Testimonies And Turn Around Breakthroughs
15. Prayers That Bring Glorious Restoration

ALSO OBTAINABLE AT

☞ **BATTLE CRY CHRISTIAN MINISTRIES**
Bookshop Shopping Mall, Prayer City
Km 12, Lagos / Ibadan Express way

☞ 2, Oregun Road, by Radio Bus Stop, Ikeja, Lagos
Km 12, Lagos / Ibadan Express way

☞ 54, Akeju Street, off Shipeolu Street, Palmgrove, Lagos

☞ Shop 26, Divine Grace Shopping Plaza, Isolo Jakande Estate, Isolo

☞ Christian Bookstores.

BOOK ORDER

Is there any book written by Dr. D. K. Olukoya (General Overseer MFM Ministries) that you would like to have? Have you seen his latest books? To place order for this end-time materials,

Text your request as follows :

Book Title(s) : . . . .

Delivery Address. : . . . .

Text to : 0816 122 9775

God bless you.

Battle Cry Christian Ministries

... equipping the saints of God

The Battle Against The Spirit Of Impossibility

Uncommon battles require uncommon warfare strategies. The new warfare strategy, which the Holy Ghost has factored, is the subject of this book. Divinely inspired, well researched, carefully written, well laced with scriptures and offered in a simple readable form, The Battle Against The Spirit Of Impossibility is one weapon which will put paid to every form of spiritual harassment. It will surely deal a decisive blow on every enemy of your progress. Careful attention to details coupled with the aggressive use of the prayer points contained in this book, will give you a permanent victory over the spirit of impossibility.

About the Author

Dr. D. K. Olukoya, is the General Overseer of the Mountain of Fire and Miracles (MFM) Ministries and The Battle Cry Christian Ministries (BCCM).

The Mountain of Fire and Miracles Ministries' Headquarters is the largest single Christian congregation in Africa with an attendance of over 120,000 at any church service

MFM is a full gospel ministry devoted to the revival of Apostolic signs, Holy Ghost Fireworks, miracles and the unlimited demonstration of the power of God to deliver to the uttermost. Absolute holiness within and without as spiritual insecticide and pre-requisite for heaven is openly taught. MFM is a do-it-yourself Gospel Ministry, where your hands are trained to wage war and your fingers to do battle.

Dr. Olukoya holds a first class honours degree in Micro-biology, from the University of Lagos and a PhD in Molecular Genetics, from the University of Reading, United Kingdom. As a researcher, he has over seventy scientific publications to his credit.

Anointed by God, Dr. Olukoya is a prophet, evangelist, teacher and preacher of the Word. His life and that of his wife, Shade and their son Elijah Toluwani are living proof that all power belong to God.

978-38233-1-0

www.ingramcontent.com/pod-product-compliance
Lightning Source LLC
Chambersburg PA
CBHW060857050426
42453CB00008B/993